DADDY PLAYS DISC GOLF

Written by Melissa Davey
Illustrated by Andrea Gijón

Copyright © 2020 Melissa Davey
All rights reserved.
No part of this book may be reproduced or used
in any manner without the prior written consent
of the copyright owner except for the use
of brief quotations in a book review.

To request permissions, contact the publisher
at rustypatchpublishing@gmail.com

ISBN: 978-1-7352714-0-8

First paperback edition October 2020.

Written by Melissa Davey
Cover Art by Andrea Gijón
Layout by Andrea Gijón
Illustrations by Andrea Gijón

Rusty Patch Publishing LLC,
Minneapolis, MN

Dedicated to Daddio and my first disc ever thrown.

DADDY PLAYS DISC GOLF

Written by Melissa Davey
Illustrated by Andrea Gijón

Daddy plays disc golf and now he's showing me.

We make a snack,
put it in our pack,
and he puts the bag
on his back.

I hold his hand and off we go,

daddy doesn't mind if we walk slow.

You play outside at a course throwing discs with great force.

At each hole there is a basket where you want your disc to be.

Warm up your throws,
go putt and play.
Enjoy life on this
fine sunny day.

When you're ready,
find the first pin.
Pick one disc to begin.

There's Zoomers, Zingers, Bouncers, and Dingers!

Pick the best disc for your throw.

Step on the tee pad and get ready to go.

Drive!

Approach!

Putt for three, make sure to throw around that tree!

Discs fly, float, and curve about.

I throw my disc then watch its route.

Daddy yells when he hits a tree but then he looks and smiles at me.

What happened?

ZOOM!

He lost a disc
he couldn't see.

Sometimes you lose one, but it's okay.

You have to remember it's a beautiful day.

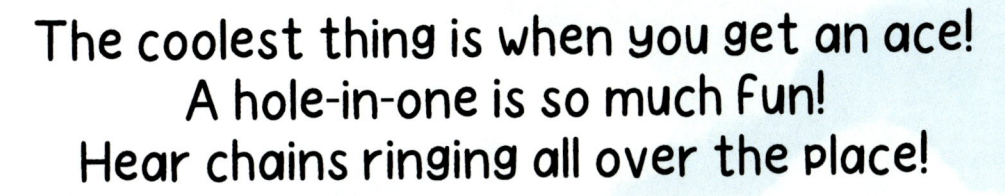

The coolest thing is when you get an ace!
A hole-in-one is so much fun!
Hear chains ringing all over the place!

Walk down the fairway
with good pace,
but don't forget it's not a race.

As you end the round,
you count your score.

Over, under,
let's play some more.

Disc golf makes me so happy, especially when I'm with my disc golfin' daddy.

Missy (Melissa) Davey
Writer

Missy is an active, dynamic mom and middle school teacher who likes to create, grow, and play outside. Introduced to disc golf in 2008 by her now husband, she frequently enjoys playing disc golf around Minnesota with her friends and family. Wanting to have a story to read at bedtime to her little one, she wrote this story to help teach her daughter about the game and hopes that it brings you joy as well!

Andrea Gijón
Illustrator

Andrea is a Mexican illustrator who enjoys nature and being surrounded by plants. She is creative and works daily to improve as a person. She hopes you enjoy this book as much as she enjoyed illustrating it.

Made in the USA
Middletown, DE
27 May 2021